M000034226

*Saint Catherine of Siena, The Story of
the Girl Who Saw Saints in the Sky*

A RACE for Heaven Study Guide

Janet P. McKenzie

Catholic Enrichment Activities
for Mary Fabyan Windeatt's

Saint Catherine of Siena, The Story of the Girl Who Saw Saints in the Sky

A RACE for Heaven Study Guide

Janet P. McKenzie

Biblio Resource Publications, Inc.
Bessemer, Michigan

© 2001, 2009 by Janet P. McKenzie

ISBN 978-1-934185-11-7

Published by
Biblio Resource Publications, Inc.
108½ South Moore Street
Bessemer, MI 49911
www.BiblioResource.com

All right reserved. No part of this book may be reproduced, stored in a retrieval system, or transmitted, in any form or by any means, electronic, mechanical, photocopying, recording, or otherwise, without the written permission of the author.

Scripture references in this work are taken from the *New American Bible with Revised New Testament* © 1986, 1970 Confraternity of Christian Doctrine, Washington, D.C.

All quotations from the Windeatt biographies are excerpted from the edition published by Tan Books and Publisher, Inc. If using the original hardback version of this book, *Saints in the Sky, The Story of Saint Catherine of Siena for Children,* note that the text will be the same but the page numbers will vary from the Tan edition.

Printed in the United States of America

Table of Contents

Spiritual Read-Aloud

Spiritual Reading

In *My Daily Bread, A Summary of the Spiritual Life* by Fr. Anthony Paone, S.J., Christ tells us,

> My Child, reading and reflecting are a great help to your spiritual life. My doctrine is explained in many books. . .Some of these books are written simply, and some are very profound and learned. Choose those which will help you most toward a greater understanding and appreciation of My Truth. Do not read to impress others but rather to be impressed yourself. Read so that you may learn My way of thinking and of doing things.

In her book, *Saint Dominic, Preacher of the Rosary and Founder of the Dominican Order*, Mary Fabyan Windeatt quotes Saint Dominic as saying, "A little good reading, much prayer and meditation. . . and God will do the rest." Father Peter-Thomas Rohrbach, O.C.D., states that spiritual reading is the "third essential asset for mediation" (after detachment and recollection). The great value he places on the habit of spiritual reading is expressed in his book *Conversation with Christ, An Introduction to Mental Prayer*:

> We live in a world devoid, in great part, of a Christian spirit, in an atmosphere and culture estranged from God. Living in such a non-theological environment makes it difficult for us to remain in contact with the person of Christ and the true purpose of life itself. We must, if we are to remain realistically attached to Christ, combat this atmosphere and surround ourselves with a new one. Constant spiritual read-

ing fills our minds with Christ and His doctrine—it creates this new climate for us.

In former ages, spiritual reading was not as essential for one's prayer life. People lived in a Christian world and culture which was reflected in their laws, customs, amusements, and their very outlook on life. This situation has radically altered in the last two hundred years, and men must now compensate for this deficit through other media, principally reading. And as the de-Christianization of our world continues, the necessity for spiritual reading simultaneously increases. We stand in need of something to bridge the gap between our pagan surroundings and our conversation with Christ—spiritual reading fills this need.

There is today in our country an alarming decline in general reading of all types. It has been estimated that in 1955 an astonishing forty-eight percent of the American adult population reads *no books at all*, and only eighteen percent read from one to four books. The decline in reading is naturally reflected in religious reading as well. And, while the lack of secular reading will occasion a decrease in culture life, the decline in religious reading will have repercussions of a more serious nature— severe detriment to one's spiritual life. Any serious attempt to better one's life spiritually should, therefore, include the resolution to engage in more spiritual reading.

If we confine our reading to non-Catholic books, magazines and newspapers, we almost automatically exclude ourselves from full development in our prayer life. The maxims and philosophy of life expressed in these avenues of communication slowly begin to seep into our lives until eventually they occupy a ruling position. We will not have surrounded ourselves with a new climate; rather, the non-Catholic climate will have engulfed us (Chapter 19).

As this decry of the "de-Christianization of our world" was written in 1956, one can safely surmise that the necessity of cultivating the habit of spiritual reading can only have grown in the past several decades.

Spiritual Read-Aloud

As supported above, spiritual reading is an essential element of every Christian's life. However, as demonstrated by the ancient practice within monasteries of spiritual read-aloud, this habit is a powerful tool for shared community growth in the spiritual life. For Catholic families, the practice of reading spiritual books aloud produces four desirable effects:

I.   It reinforces the habit of spiritual reading for each member of the family and allows each member to practice this habit regardless of age

II. It reinforces the habit of spiritual conversation if the reading results in even a general discussion of the values and virtues being portrayed in the story

III. It strengthens the family as the domestic Church where members exist to learn and live the Faith together for the support and enrichment of all family members

IV. It allows the discussion and demonstration of the practical application of the Faith for all age levels

The Habit of Spiritual Reading

As outlined above, establishing the habit of daily spiritual reading is essential to our spiritual growth. Through read-aloud, children can be taught at an early age that daily spiritual reading is a fun, rewarding exercise. Do make this time together pleasant by allowing the children to do crafts, draw, play quietly with puzzles, toys, etc. As long as their attention is not divided and they can participate in a discussion of the reading afterwards, allow quiet activity. One cannot expect children to sit piously with hands clasped prayerfully during the entire read-aloud session. As the children get older, encourage them to read other spiritual books, including the Bible, during a quiet time of their own. Model this habit by allowing them to observe your habit of daily spiritual reading as well. Although the family read-aloud sessions may be as long as thirty minutes, private spiritual reading times may be considerably shorted depending on the habits and temperament of each child.

The Habit of Spiritual Conversation

This habit, for many families, may begin with spiritual read-aloud. When each member of the family participates in a spiritual discussion of a religious book, the practice of discussing matters of faith and Christ-like living begins to form. If the formation of holy habits and imitation of the saints is the goal, these discussions will become commonplace in the home as each member checks the others on their actions and words. As family members become more comfortable and open about spiritual matters, this practice will soon spread into other areas of their lives. Spiritual discussions with friends and other relatives will become more natural and in fact become important topics to be discussed. Sharing one's own spirituality and encouraging others to become more open about matter of faith will then become an integral pattern of living.

Strengthening the Domestic Church

As we read more about the saints and their lives and begin to share our faith more openly with others, we realize the importance of holy companionship—living with others who share our faith ideas and supporting each other in our attempts to become more like Christ. Families begin to growth together in their knowledge of the Catholic faith and become more willing to support each other throughout the ups and downs of community living. We begin to "bear one another's burdens with peace and harmony and unselfishness." Just as Christ has His Church to help bring salvation to all, we—as family members—have each other to provide mutual support and encouragement in our efforts to enter the narrow gate. Within our families, we can create the Catholic culture that is missing from our world's culture.

The Practical Application of the Faith for All Ages

When lives of the saints are read aloud in the family setting, all aged children can participate in a discussion of the imitation of the saint's virtues and holy habits. Each member can help others understand how to apply the lessons the saints teach us on a practical level. All family members can help choose a particular habit or virtue upon which to focus. A reward system can be established for virtuous behavior. A family "plan of attack" on non-virtuous habits and attitudes can be developed, implemented, checked, and revised. All family members can be encouraged and taught how to imitate Christ by the imitation of His saints.

Summary

Regular family read-aloud sessions that center around the lives of the saints will benefit the family with an increased interest in reading—especially saintly literature—a growth in vocabulary, and an improved sense of family unity. Additionally, family members will be encouraged to develop the habit of spiritual reading on their own, will become more comfortable and experienced with spiritual conversation, and be able to apply the Truths of the Catholic faith on a practical level to all aspects of their lives—no matter what their age. The customs, habits, and attitudes of the family will more and more reflect those of the Catholic culture. Perseverance in this simple daily ritual will help to "bridge the gap between our pagan surroundings and our conversation with Christ."

When Mother Reads Aloud

When Mother reads aloud the past
Seems real as every day;
I hear the tramp of armies vast,
I see the spears and lances cast,
I join the thrilling fray;
Brave knights and ladies fair and proud
I meet when Mother reads aloud.

When Mother reads aloud, far lands
Seem very near and true;
I cross the desert's gleaming sands,
Or hunt the jungle's prowling bands,
Or sail the ocean blue;
Far heights, whose peaks the cold mists shroud,
I scale, when Mother reads aloud.

When Mother reads aloud I long
For noble deeds to do—
To help the right, redress the wrong,
It seems so easy to be strong, so simple to be true,
O, thick and fast the visions crowd
When Mother reads aloud.

—Anonymous

The Reading Mother

I had a mother who read to me
Sagas of pirates who scoured the sea,
Cutlasses clenched in their yellow teeth,
"Blackbirds" stowed in the hold beneath.

I had a mother who read me plays
Of ancient and gallant and golden days
Stories of Marmion and Ivanhoe,
Which every boy has a right to know.

I had a mother who read me tales
Of Gelert the hound of the hills of Wales,
True to his trust till his tragic death,
Faithfulness blest with his final breath.

I had a mother who read me things
That wholesome life to the boy-heart brings—
Stories that stir with an upward touch,
O, that each mother of boys were such.

You may have tangible wealth untold,
Caskets of jewels and coffers of gold.
Richer than I you can never be—
I had a mother who read to me.

–Strickland Gullilan

How to Use This Study Guide

REVIEW Vocabulary

Vocabulary words are listed at the beginning of each lesson. Words on the left are secular words and are given within the sentence structure. Vocabulary words listed in the right-hand column are Catholic vocabulary words. Allow students to guess the meaning of the italicized word before looking it up. This helps them to surmise the meaning from context, a skill that enhances reading comprehension and strengthens vocabulary. Help students identify any suffixes, prefixes or root words that might give clues to the word's meaning. If still unable to define a word, use a dictionary. For Catholic vocabulary words, use RACE for Heaven's *The Windeatt Dictionary.*

??? Comprehension Questions/Narration Prompts

These questions are appropriate for all age levels. They can be used several ways, depending on a student's ability. For students with difficulty in reading comprehension, read and briefly discuss these questions before reading the chapter. Discuss, too, the sub-title provided under each chapter heading in the study guide. The student will then know what content to watch for within the reading. If read afterward, the questions become a *test of,* rather than an *aid to,* comprehension. For students with adequate comprehension skills, use the questions for oral review to insure that important content has been absorbed.

Use these questions too as prompts for narration, which is simply the oral retelling of the story in the student's own words. It is a helpful tool to determine the level of each student's comprehension. All ages may benefit from the practice of narration. If done within a mixed age group, begin with the youngest students and have the older students add details to the already-related story.

Answers to comprehension questions are provided in the answer key.

Forming Opinions/Drawing Conclusions

More than relating events, these questions require the student to develop an opinion, or to uncover or discover material not expressly stated in the text. They are designed to develop thinking skills and do not usually require the use of any outside resources. Use this section with children grades four and up as the basis for discussion or as a writing assignment.

 For Further Study

Appropriate for upper elementary through high school students, this section requires the use of additional reference materials. These activities invite students to look more deeply at the historical events and people that shaped the times of each character. Topics in this section may be used for oral presentations or written reports.

 Growing in Holiness

These activities are different from the others in that they do not involve discussion or study as much as personal action and interior reflection. They can perhaps be considered "conversion activities" or "life lessons." By applying the spiritual lessons of the story to everyday life, the student is encouraged to develop habits in imitation of the saints—which is an imitation of Christ Himself. Remember to reinforce these activities with the student and to comment when they are observed in action.

**Geography**

The map provided with this study guide serves to orient the students with respect to space—*where* the action of the story is taking place—as well as to acquaint them with common geographical landmarks. Permission is hereby granted to photocopy maps for family or classroom use.

Timeline Work

The creation of a timeline allows students to place the story's events within a wider historical framework. Simple directions for making a timeline are included in the study guide. Students will need plain paper, colored markers or pencils, and a ruler.

✓ Checking the Catechism

For older students, these activities will require a copy of the *Catechism of the Catholic Church (CCC)* or its *Compendium*. The references for the more concise *Compendium* appear in parentheses after the *CCC* citations. Older students can read aloud—and then discuss—the stated text paragraphs with an adult.

For younger students, use any grade-appropriate catechism to review the doctrines and terms as specified. An excellent activity book for multi-grades is Ignatius Press' *100 Activities Based on the Catechism of the Catholic Church* by Ellen Rossini. Discuss together how the specific topics from the catechism are illustrated in the thoughts and actions of the characters in the book.

Searching Scripture

Familiarize the student with the inspired Word of God by studying the biblical passages as provided. Strengthen these exercises by occasionally requiring memorization of the verse(s). Stress that knowledge of Scripture is an important part of our faith education.

Note that Ms. Windeatt used the Douay-Rheims translation of the Bible, which was the translation in use in the United States until 1970 when it was replaced by the New American Bible in the *Lectionary of Mass*. The Douay-Rheims translation is taken from the Latin Vulgate, whereas the New American translation comes from the original languages of Hebrew, Aramaic or Greek (as the case may be for each specific book). For this reason, some of the books' names (as well as some of the Psalms' numbers) differ between these two translations. When these differences occur in the biblical citiations within this study guide, the New American references are given first with the Douay-Rheims references following in parentheses. All biblical references used in this study guide are from the New American translation.

 Test

The purpose of the test is to ensure that the student has comprehended the important events in each saint's life as well as the lessons the story intends to impart. An answer key is provided for these questions.

In addition to the test, many students will benefit from the completion of a book report. See RACE for Heaven's *Alternative Book Reports for Catholic Students* for additional information on book reports specifically geared to saint biographies. Consider requiring each student to choose one of these reports or activities upon completion of the Windeatt biography.

Warning

These study guides are comprehensive. They contain activities for a variety of age levels and areas of study. Do **not** attempt to complete every activity for every lesson. Do only those exercises that are suitable for the needs of your current situation. Resist the impulse to be so thorough that the story line of the book is lost, and the read-aloud sessions become dreaded rather than anticipated. This study guide is meant to enhance your reading—not to become the dictating tyrant of your read-aloud time together. If you are reading to young audiences, consider just using the comprehension and opinion questions as well as the "Growing in Holiness" section; use the maps as a geographical visual aid. Re-read the books to complete the more advanced activities in later years. Another suggestion is to use the activities designed for older students in coordination with their history, geography, writing and/or religious curriculum. This study guide could also be used as a complete unit study for hectic times when regular school may not be in session such as Advent, times of family stress (the birth of a new sibling, for example) or over the summer months. By reading the book and completing many of the activities, subjects such as religion, reading, writing, geography, and history can all be easily covered. The most important rules to the successful use of this study guide are

1. Be creative rather than obsessive

2. Be flexible rather than overly structured

3. Enjoy!

Saint Catherine of Siena

In Siena, Italy, as a young girl,
She saw saints in the sky like pictures unfurl.
She tried to flee,
A hermit to be,
She offered up much—even cut off her curl.

Catherine lived like a maid in her own family's house.
No husband for her—God was her loved spouse.
More saints did she see.
She wanted to be
Not a nun, but live in the world, in her house.

She prayed hard for sinners, lived in a small room,
Caught smallpox, and 'fore the disease did consume,
To Dominic she went—
Her mom gave her consent—
She joined the order, a habit to assume.

God gave her His ring as her worthy reward
For honoring Him as her God and her Lord—
Lived in the world still,
The Lord's Will to fulfill,
Moved back with her fam'ly, her maid's life restored.

She took care of lepers and young men in jail.
She bathed them and fed them, God's Will helped prevail.
For others pain bore,
To her was no chore.
For sinners she suffered each day without fail.

In the summer into France to the pope she did go.
His Avignon residence was wrong she did know.
Her persuasion did win—
Back to Rome again.
Four years later, she finished her time here below.

Think what you can learn from this saint and her tale.
How you can apply it to help you prevail.
Then mold what you do
And boldly pursue
Her pattern of holiness. Follow her trail.

Timeline of Events

Year	Event
1270	Marco Polo journeys to China; Phillip III becomes king of France
1274	Death of Saint Thomas Aquinas
1291	End of crusades
1309-1377	Papacy moved from Rome to Avignon, France, for reign of seven popes (Babylonian Captivity)
1322	Birth of Imelda Lambertini (died in 1333)
1324	Death of Marco Polo
1328	England acknowledges Scotland's independence
1337-1453	Hundred Years' War between France and England
1345	Aztecs arrive in central Mexico
1347	Birth of Catherine of Siena
1347-1353	Black Death (Bubonic Plague) sweeps Europe
1353	Catherine's first vision of saints
1359	Catherine cuts her hair and lives as a servant in her parents' home
1361	Black Death reappears in England
1363	Catherine receives the Dominican habit as a tertiary and receives an invisible ring from our Lord (spiritual marriage)
1368	Death of Catherine's father; restoration of the Great Wall of China
1369	John Hus born (died in 1415)
1370	Steel crossbow used in battle
1375	War breaks out between Pope Gregory XI and the Republic of Florence; Catherine acts as a dove of peace

1376	Catherine visits Pope Gregory XI in Avignon in the summer; September 13th, Pope Gregory XI leaves for Rome; John Wycliffe calls for reform in the Church
1377	January 17th, Pope Gregory XI arrives in Rome to end Church's "Babylonian Captivity"
1378-1417	Great Schism begins with election of both Pope Urban VI and Clement VII
1380	Death of Catherine of Siena
1387-1400	Geoffrey Chaucer writes "Canterbury Tales"
1396	Birth of Johann Gutenberg, the inventor of printing in Europe
1409	Council of Pisa called in attempt to end Great Schism
1412	Birth of Joan of Arc
1414	General Council of the Church at Constance, ending Great Schism and reforming the Church; Thomas á Kempis writes Imitation of Christ
1461	Canonization of Saint Catherine (declared a Doctor of Church in 1970)

A Map of the World of Saint Catherine of Siena

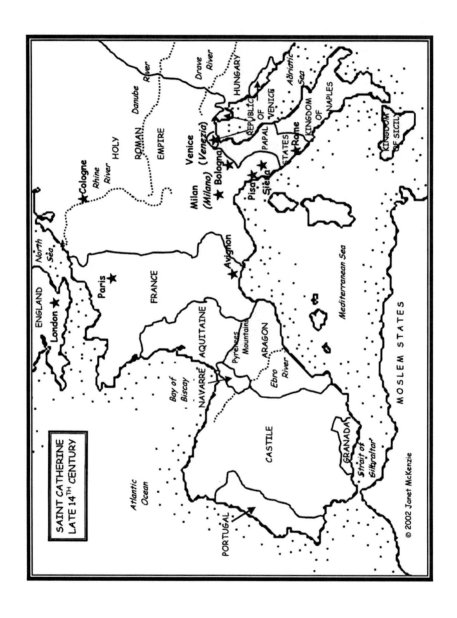

Study Guide for

Saint Catherine of Siena, The Story of the Girl Who Saw Saints in the Sky

Chapter 1–In Which Catherine Sees a Vision of Saints in the Sky

⚡REVIEW⚡ Vocabulary

Why are you so *fidgety*   *Dominican*
Who was *inclined* to be cross   *Vision*

 Comprehension Questions/Narration Prompts

1. What did Lapa want for her youngest daughter?
2. How old was Catherine when she first saw saints in the sky? Who did she see?

 Forming Opinions/Drawing Conclusions

1. What does Lapa's insistence that Catherine and Stefano not stop to visit in the Church tell you about the customary habits of Catherine as a young child?
2. Explain Catherine's thoughts regarding the difficulty of becoming a saint amidst the noise and bustle of home (page 10). Do you agree? Explain your answer.

✝ Growing in Holiness

Two references are made in this chapter to Jesus in the Blessed Sacrament—the first when Lapa cautions the children not to stop for a visit at the church and the second when Stefano chides Catherine for seeing our Lord above the church when He is in the church. Make more visits to our Lord in the Blessed Sacrament to pray. Remember His presence whenever you are in church and whenever you receive Him in Holy Communion. If you are not able to visit our Lord in the tabernacle, make frequent spiritual communions with Him. (See the answer key at the end of this study guide for more information on making a spiritual communion.)

Timeline Work

Taping sheets of plain paper end-to-end, make a timeline representing the years from 1270 through 1461. Let three inches equal 25 years. Mark on your timeline the dates and events from 1270 through 1353, using information from pages xvi-xvii of this study guide.

Searching Scripture

1. Review the shades of the rainbow that Jacopo used as a model for his dyes. Read the story of God's covenant with man as sealed by the sign of the rainbow in Genesis 9:8-17. Read also Sirach 43:12-13 (Ecclesiasticus 43:11-12) regarding the rainbow.

2. All the saints Catherine saw in the vision are in the Bible. Read in the Bible about these three saints. Why did these particular saints appear to Catherine?

Chapter 2–In Which Catherine Runs Away to Become a Hermit

✯REVIEW✯ Vocabulary
In the *cobbled* street   *hermit*
Nearby *hovered* a guardian angel   *saint*

??? Comprehension Questions/Narration Prompts
1. Why did Catherine decide to run away from home?
2. What did our Lord tell Catherine that her life's work was to be?
3. When she decided to return home, Catherine prayed. How quickly was her prayer answered and in what way?
4. Why did Stefano find it hard to believe all that Catherine told him?

Forming Opinions/Drawing Conclusions
List three activities or habits that you can begin or change that would help you start becoming a saint in your own home.

Growing in Holiness
We cannot all become hermits and run away whenever we need time with God. Recall that Jesus often went off to be alone with God and pray. Discuss the possibility of the entire family having a day of quiet prayer. Remember to maintain a peaceful atmosphere all day with time for both individual and family prayer. Use candles, soft music, and incense to create a more prayerful atmosphere.

🧭 Geography

Trace the map on page xviii of this study guide. Color these seas and oceans blue: Atlantic, North, Adriatic, and Mediterranean as well as these rivers: Rhine, Danube, Ebro, and Drave. The remainder of the map will be completed in Chapter 7.

✓ Checking the Catechism

Older students should read text paragraphs 897-933, 1593, 1597, and 1660 (188-193, 325, and 535) in the *Catechism of the Catholic Church* (*CCC*) on the vocations of lay people and the consecrated life. If desired, complete Activity #55 in *100 Activities*. Remember to pray daily to discern God's unique plan for you.

📖 Searching Scripture

1. Re-read the conversation between Stefano and Catherine found on page 17. Then read Matthew 13:57. Why is it hard to believe that saints and prophets live among us?
2. John the Baptist lived alone in the desert—Matthew 3:1-6. Also read about Saint Paul's three years in the desert in Galatians 1:15-18.

Chapter 3–In Which Catherine Takes Drastic Measures to Avoid Marriage

✦REVIEW✦ Vocabulary

daughter's *cropped* head

not inclined to hold a *grudge*

mercy

disciples

??❓ Comprehension Questions/Narration Prompts

1. Relate the story of Catherine's hair and why she cut it.
2. How was Catherine punished for this?
3. What plan did Catherine devise to make her new work more pleasant?

💡 Forming Opinions/Drawing Conclusions

1. Think of how you handled your punishment when disciplined recently. How does your attitude compare with Catherine's attitude toward her punishment?
2. Describe Catherine's plan to think of her family as the Holy Family of Nazareth. How can you incorporate this plan into your daily living?
3. Christians are often criticized for having "odd ideas"—such as not caring about money, personal looks, or powerful positions. Do you think it was wrong that Catherine did not wish to marry and help her family financially? Explain your answer.

For Further Study

The church in Siena was a Dominican church; Catherine's stepbrother, Father Thomas della Fonte, was a Dominican priest. Research the history of the Dominican order, which was a relatively new order at the time of Catherine's life.

✝ **Growing in Holiness**

While Catherine's punishment may seem severe, you can do much in your family to help out without becoming a Cinderella. Do at least two chores around the house each day without being asked. Offer them up to Jesus in reparation for sins. Be sure not to seek any praise, reward, or even recognition for these acts.

✓ **Checking the Catechism**

Older students should read text paragraphs 2197-2207 (455-458) in the *CCC* on the domestic church. If desired, complete Activity #57 in *100 Activities*.

📖 **Searching Scripture**

While there is not much information on the life of the Holy Family in the Bible, you can read of Jesus' submission to His parents in Luke 2:41-52.

Chapter 4–In Which Saint Dominic Appears to Catherine

 Vocabulary

In the *somber* black
saw each one of them *beckon to her*

religious orders
religious family

 Comprehension Questions/Narration Prompts

1. The second time Catherine saw saints in the sky she recognized more of them. Name the six saints she saw.
2. What was the message that Saint Dominic gave to Catherine?

 Forming Opinions/Drawing Conclusions

1. Why do you think God allowed Jacopo to see the dove above his daughter when he found her at prayer?
2. What you think is God's plan for Catherine's life? Quote statements from the book to support your argument.

For Further Study

Briefly research each of the six saints in Catherine's vision. Review how each of them is portrayed in pictures so that you too might recognize them.

Growing in Holiness

Jocopo found Catherine kneeling in her room praying just as Jesus has asked us to pray (Matthew 6:6) and just as Daniel prayed in Daniel 6:11 (6:10-11). "Her heart was full of gratitude" (page 27). Remember when you pray to not just use the most common form of prayer—petition or asking God for various things—but also to use the other four forms of prayer: adoration of God, intercession or praying for others, thanksgiving, and praise of God. Try to make your prayers less asking and more thanking, praising, and thinking of others.

 Timeline Work

Add the dates and events from 1359 through 1370 to your timeline.

Older students can read text paragraphs 222-27, 795, 1167, 1328, and 2637-38 (43, 67, 221, 443, 547, 550, and 555) in the *CCC* on giving thanks. If desired, complete Activity #66 in *100 Activities*. Read too the citations in the *CCC* from St. Catherine's *Dialogue* in text paragraphs 313, 356, and 1937.

Chapter 5–In Which Catherine Receives the Dominican Habit

✦REVIEW✦ Vocabulary

in this tiny *chamber*

smallpox plague

Tertiary

Ash Wednesday

 Comprehension Questions/Narration Prompts

1. At the age of sixteen, what did Catherine decide her life work was to be? What did she do because of this decision?
2. Catherine needed her mother in order to implement the second step of her plan. What did she request her mother to do? Did her mother agree to do it?
3. What did God do to help Catherine in her plan to become a Dominican tertiary?
4. What did Catherine predict regarding her mother's future?
5. Who taught Catherine to read and write?
6. What saints did Catherine see in her third vision?
7. What did our Lord say to Catherine when he placed the invisible ring on her finger? How old was Catherine?

 Forming Opinions/Drawing Conclusions

What does "a religious with the whole world for her convent" (page 36) mean?

For Further Study

Briefly research each of the five saints of Catherine's third vision. Be sure to find pictures of each saint so that you can recognize their faces.

✝ Growing in Holiness

Catherine speaks of her life's work—suffering for sinners and their sins. Think of a sinner from the news or from your own life and offer all of your sacrifices for the next week for this person. Offer prayers, fast from a certain food or pleasure, make visits to Jesus in the tabernacle, and secretly do extra chores.

✓ Checking the Catechism

Older students should read in the *CCC* text paragraphs 1434-38, 2041-43, 2174-76, and 2180-88 (241, 276, 289, 291, 301, 432, 450-454, 567) regarding two of the commandments of the Church—our obligation regarding Sunday Mass and the Church's laws on fasting.

📖 Searching Scripture

"The prophet David began to play sweet music on his little harp" (page 39). Read the beginning of the story of David in 1 Samuel (Kings) 16:11-18:5.

Chapter 6–In Which Catherine Tends to the Sick and Converts Sinners

✴REVIEW✴ Vocabulary

to into *rapture* for joy   *sanctifying grace*
die on the *gallows*   *Purgatory*

??? Comprehension Questions/Narration Prompts

1. What did our Lord request of Catherine after giving her the invisible ring?
2. Other than again being the family's servant, what other duties did Catherine assume?
3. Catherine contracted the disease of leprosy while tending the sick. What were her first and second thoughts after being miraculously cured of this disease?
4. What did Catherine's sufferings and prayers for the convicted criminal gain?
5. What offering did Catherine make on behalf of her dying father?

 For Further Study

1. Research the disease of leprosy and write a brief report. In addition to general information on the disease itself, be sure to include information such as its current treatment and treatment in Jesus' and Catherine's time, its current rate of occurrence, and its rate of occurrence in both Jesus' and Catherine's time. Is leprosy still an incurable disease? Find two biblical passages which deal with cases of leprosy.
2. Mysticism refers to the state of the soul in which God is known in a way that no human effort could produce. Research the degrees of mystical contemplation—union with God—as outlined by Saint Teresa of Avila: the two nights of the soul (sense and spirit) before mystical un-

ion, the prayer of quiet, full union, ecstasy, and spiritual marriage or transforming union (as illustrated by Catherine in this chapter). Mysticism is not restricted to a privileged few. God wants every soul to be completely united with Him.

✠ Growing in Holiness

Perform at least three corporal works of mercy and three spiritual works of mercy within the next week.

✓ Checking the Catechism

Older students may review the teachings of the *CCC* on the works of mercy in text paragraph 2447 (520) and the beatitudes in text paragraphs 1716-29 (359-362). Younger students may review the spiritual and corporal works of mercy, and the Beatitudes in their catechisms. If desired, complete Activity #20 in *100 Activities*.

📖 Searching Scripture

Read Matthew 25:31-46. Also read these passages related to mysticism: Psalm 27 (26): 4-5, Psalm 63 (62), Psalm 73 (72): 25-26, 2 Corinthians 3:18, and 1 Peter 1:8.

Chapter 7–In Which Catherine Travels to See the Holy Father

✺REVIEW✺ Vocabulary

invasion by the *Turks*

in a kind of *trance*

Vatican

cardinals

 Comprehension Questions/Narration Prompts

1. Catherine bore the stigmata of Christ (pierced hands, side, and feet) for five years. At what age did she receive the invisible stigmata of Christ?
2. Why did Catherine decide to travel to Avignon, France—walking if necessary?

 Forming Opinions/Drawing Conclusions

1. "A woman's place is in the home" (page 52). Comment on this statement considering Catherine's vocation as given to her by our Lord.
2. Catherine asked that wise words be put in her mouth whenever she met sinners so that she could bring them to God. What "wise words" would you say to convert sinners?

 For Further Study

1. Research the Papal Palace in Avignon, France. How many years did the popes reside there? Which popes resided there? Why were they there?
2. Research the political climate at this time. Study the Turks and their invasion of the European continent at this time. Where were they from? What did they wish to accomplish? Why did they hate the Christians? What is the "terrible war" that is mentioned at the beginning of Chapter 8?

✛ Growing in Holiness

If it has been more than a month since your last reception of the Sacrament of Penance and Reconciliation (Confession), plan on participating in this sacrament within the next two weeks.

Geography

Complete the map started in Chapter 2 by labeling the cities red and the countries green. On the map provided, cities are indicated with a star, and countries are in capital letters. Using a modern map, find the current country to which each city now belongs.

✓ Checking the Catechism

Priests followed Catherine around as she instilled contrition and the need to go to confession in many people. Older students may read these text paragraphs in the *CCC:* 980, 1422, 1440, and 1448-49 (200 and 296-311) on the Sacrament of Penance and Reconciliation while younger students review this topic in their own catechisms. Complete Activity #90 in *100 Activities.*

Chapter 8–In Which Catherine Persuades the Holy Father to Return the Papacy to Rome

 Vocabulary

cloaks of *ermine*

he saw that Catherine *winced*

pope

catechism

 Comprehension Questions/Narration Prompts

1. Why did Catherine feel that the Holy Father should return to Rome?
2. Other than talk to the Holy Father (Pope Gregory XI), what else did Catherine do in her efforts to get the pope to return to Rome?
3. What convinced Pope Gregory XI to return to Rome?

 Forming Opinions/Drawing Conclusions

Why did Catherine not want the Holy Father to see Christ's wounds on her hands?

For Further Study

Research the pontificate of Gregory XI who reigned as pope from January 1371 to March 1378. At the urging of Catherine, he left Avignon in September 1376 but did not arrive in Rome until January 1377. Find out why.

Growing in Holiness

As Catherine prayed to the Holy Spirit when she had a difficult task ahead of her, so too must we pray for the Holy Spirit's guidance in our lives. Ask for the assistance of the Holy Spirit whenever you are unsure about what to do or say. It may be a simple aspiration such as "Come. Holy Spirit, come." Pray too that our pope will always be guided by the Holy Spirit.

✓ Checking the Catechism

Catherine talks of Rome as the city of Saint Peter, the first pope. Younger students should study the offices of pope and bishop as well as the mission of the apostles in their catechisms. Older students may read text paragraphs 857-62 (174-176 and 179-187) in the *CCC* on the apostolic Church. If desired, complete Activity #48 in *100 Activities*.

📖 Searching Scripture

Read Matthew 28:19-20. This mission to teach and baptize was given to the apostles and may have been part of the message that Catherine gave to Gregory XI. Also read Matthew 16:13-20 regarding our first pope.

Chapter 9–In Which Catherine's Suffering Ends

 Vocabulary

Catherine *beseeched* Our Lord   *Last Sacraments*

 Comprehension Questions/Narration Prompts

1. What two promises did Jesus make to Catherine regarding her family?
2. Why did Catherine think of herself a failure?
3. In what important aspect was Catherine not a failure?

 Forming Opinions/Drawing Conclusions

Applying what you have learned about Saint Catherine in this book, explain the accomplishments, attitudes, or habits that contributed to her canonization as a saint.

For Further Study

1. Research the procedure for electing a pope. Include the changes made in the eleventh century, those made by the Third Council of the Lateran in 1179, and those made in 1975 by Pope Paul VI. Who is eligible to become pope? Determine who nominates and who votes. Can the pope be removed from office or resign? (Use Laux's *Church History*, Johnson's *The Story of the Church*, or search on the Internet.)
2. Saint Catherine's holiness and learning—as displayed in her life and her *Dialogue*—prompted the Church to confer upon her the honorary title of "Doctor of the Church" in 1970. Read more about the Doctors of the Catholic Church on pages 19-20 below. What other saints in the Windeatt biography series have been given this title? Research the life of one of the Church's Doctors.

Growing in Holiness

Memorize one or more of the following aspirations to be recited after receiving Holy Communion: "O Jesus in the Blessed Sacrament, have mercy on us." "Eucharistic Heart of Jesus, increase my faith, hope, and love." "Sacred Heart of Jesus, may You be known, may You be loved, may You be imitated." "Heart of Jesus burning with love for me, inflame my heart with love for Thee." "O my God and my all, may the sweet flame of Your love consume my soul, that I may die to the world for the love of You, who has died on the cross for love of me."

Timeline Work

Add the events from 1375 through 1461 to complete your timeline.

Searching Scripture

Regarding Catherine's inedia (ability to live on the Eucharist as the sole source of food and drink), read John 4:31-34. Read too John 6:48-59.

Doctors of the Catholic Church

The title of "Doctor of the Church," a title originally conferred on the four great Western Fathers of the Church—Gregory the Great, Ambrose, Augustine, and Jerome—is bestowed upon those canonized saints of the Church whose writing and/or preaching is outstanding in guiding the faithful. The Doctors of the Church are recognized for their learning and holiness of life. Listed below are the Doctors, the dates they lived, and the year they were given the title of "Doctor of the Church."

1. Saint Athanasius – c. 297-373 (prior to 750)
2. Saint Ephrem or Ephraem of Syria – c. 306-c. 373 (1920)
3. Saint Cyril of Jerusalem – c. 315-386 (1882)
4. Saint Hilary of Poitiers – c. 315-c. 368 (1851)
5. Saint Gregory Nazianzen or Gregory of Nazianzus – c. 329-c. 389 (prior to 750)
6. Saint Basil the Great – c. 329-379 (prior to 750)
7. Saint Ambrose – c. 340–397 (prior to 750)
8. Saint Jerome – c. 342-c. 420 (prior to 750)
9. Saint John Chrysostom – c. 347-407 (prior to 750)
10. Saint Augustine – 354-430 (prior to 750)
11. Saint Cyril of Alexandria – c. 376-444 (1882)
12. Pope Saint Leo the Great – c. 400-461 (1574)
13. Saint Peter Chrysologus – c. 406 –c. 450 (1729)
14. Pope Saint Gregory the Great - c. 540-604 (prior to 750)
15. Saint Isidore of Seville – c. 560-636 (1722)
16. Saint Bede the Venerable – c. 673-735 (1899)
17. Saint John Damascene or John of Damascus) – c. 676-c. 749 (1890)
18. Saint Peter Damian – c. 1007-1072 (1828)
19. Saint Anselm of Canterbury– 1033-1109 (1720)

20. Saint Bernard of Clairvaux – c. 1090-1153 (1830)
21. Saint Anthony of Padua – 1195-1231 (1946)
22. Saint Albert the Great – c. 1206-1280 (1931)
23. Saint Bonaventure – c. 1221-1274 (1588)
24. Saint Thomas Aquinas – c. 1225-1274 (1568)
25. Saint Catherine of Siena – 1347-1380 (1970)
26. Saint Teresa of Avila – 1515-1582 (1970)
27. Saint Peter Canisius – 1521-1597 (1925)
28. Saint Robert Bellarmine – 1542-1621 (1931)
29. Saint John of the Cross – 1542-1591 (1926)
30. Saint Lawrence of Brindisi – 1559-1619 (1959)
31. Saint Francis de Sales – 1567-1622 (1877)
32. Saint Alphonsus Liguori – 1696-1787 (1871)
33. Saint Therese of Lisieux – 1873-1897 (1997)

Book Summary Test and Answer Key for

Saint Catherine of Siena, The Story of the Girl Who Saw Saints in the Sky

Book Summary Test for *St. Catherine of Siena*

Directions: Answer in complete sentences. 100 possible points, 20 points for each answer.

1. Name at least three miracles attributed to Catherine in her lifetime.

   _____

   _____

   _____

   _____

2. To what religious order did Catherine belong?

   _____

   _____

3. Describe the daily life of Catherine in her late teens and twenties.

   _____

   _____

   _____

   _____

4. What did Catherine accomplish when she traveled to France?

_____

_____

_____

_____

_____

_____

5. Saint Catherine of Siena shows us that it is not necessary to become a priest or cloistered nun to achieve holiness. How can we become holy even in the midst of the distractions of daily family life? What habits are important? What information and practices will aid in our quest to increase our holiness?

_____

_____

_____

_____

_____

_____

_____

_____

St. Catherine Siena, The Story of the Girl Who Saw Saints in the Sky
Answer Key to Comprehension Questions

Chapter 1—In Which Catherine Sees a Vision of Saints in the Sky

1. Lapa wanted Catherine to grow up to be beautiful and marry a rich man, so Lapa and her husband could enlarge their shop.
2. Catherine was six when she first saw a vision of saints in the sky. She recognized Christ the King and some of the others as John the Baptist, Saint Peter, and Saint Paul.

Growing In Holiness

The Council of Trent, held in the sixteenth century, asked all the faithful to make a spiritual communion on the days that they do not receive Holy Communion. Saint Alphonsus Liguori advised us to make a spiritual communion at least three times a day—in the morning, at noon, and in the evening. Our Lord appeared to Sister Benigna Consolata of Como, Italy, in 1916 and said, "Make as many spiritual communions as possible to supply for the many sacramental communions which are not made. One every quarter of an hour is not enough. Make them shorter, but more numerous." One spiritual communion prayer follows: "My Jesus, I believe that You are present in the Most Holy Eucharist. I love You above all things, and I desire to receive You into my soul. Since I cannot at this moment receive You sacramentally, come at least spiritually into my heart. I embrace You as if You were already here and unite myself wholly to You. Never permit me to be separated from You." You may also memorize a shorter form—"I believe that You are in the most holy Sacrament. I love You and desire You. Come into my heart. I embrace You; never leave me!" Alternatively, memorize a spiritual communion prayer of your own creation.

Chapter 2—In Which Catherine Runs Away to Become a Hermit

1. Catherine felt she could not be a saint among the hustle and bustle of her home, so she decided to run away and become a hermit in a cave.
2. Jesus told Catherine that her life's work was to live in the world and bring others to Christ. Jesus told her that He has need of saints who live in families.
3. Catherine's prayer was answered immediately as she miraculously traveled from the cave to her home instantaneously.
4. As Stefano didn't feel Catherine was capable of walking that far out into the country, he didn't believe the rest of her story either. He also did not believe that miracles were happening to Catherine as he saw her as a very ordinary person—his sister.

Chapter 3—In Which Catherine Takes Measures to Avoid Marriage

1. When she reached the age of twelve, Catherine's parents begin to speak to her about marriage. Catherine did not want to marry as she wished to live alone with God for her entire life. So Catherine went to see her stepbrother, a Dominican priest, for advice. He suggested that she cut off her hair to make herself unattractive. Catherine did as he suggested even though he told her that her parents would be furious.
2. Catherine was given all the jobs of the servant girl as punishment for the hair cutting.
3. Catherine's plan was to think of her father as Saint Joseph, her mother as the Blessed Mother, and her brothers and sisters as our Lord's disciples. All the work she did for her family was now done for her heavenly family.

Chapter 4—In Which Saint Dominic Appears to Catherine

1. In her second vision of saints, Catherine saw Sts. Benedict, Francis of Assisi, Augustine, Norbert, Bernard, and Dominic.

2. Saint Dominic approached Catherine with the habit of his order in his arms and told her that one day she would wear this habit.

Chapter 5—In Which Catherine Receives the Dominican Habit

1. At the age of sixteen, Catherine decided that her life work was to pray and suffer for sinners. She requested the smallest room in the house and decided to confine herself to this room, leaving only to go to Mass and the Sacrament of Penance and Reconciliation (Confession).
2. Catherine requested that her mother go to the Dominicans to ask on her behalf that Catherine be admitted as a Dominican tertiary. Her mother refused to go.
3. God allowed Catherine to become very ill with smallpox in order to fulfill His Holy Will.
4. Catherine predicted that her mother would someday become a Dominican tertiary too.
5. Our Lord Himself miraculously taught Catherine to read and write.
6. The third time Catherine had a vision of saints she saw the Blessed Virgin, Saint John the Evangelist, Saint Paul, King David, and Saint Dominic.
7. When He placed the invisible ring upon her finger Our Lord said to Catherine, "I take you for my own chosen one" (page 39). Catherine was nineteen years old.

Chapter 6—In Which Catherine Tends to the Sick and Converts Sinners

1. Our Lord asked Catherine to go back to live with her family—no longer to live by herself in her room but to go back into the world.
2. Catherine began to go out to help the sick and the poor by bringing them clothes and food, and nursing them if they were ill.
3. Catherine's first thought after her cure was to thank God for His goodness. Secondly, she was grateful that she could no longer pass the disease to her family.
4. Because of Catherine's suffering and prayers, the criminal agreed to see a priest and go to Confession before his death. She saved his soul from hell.

5. Catherine agreed to bear herself any suffering her father should have had, which then allowed him to go straight to heaven. Catherine suffered pain the rest of her life because of this agreement.

Chapter 7—In Which Catherine Travels to See the Holy Father

1. Catherine received the stigmata of Christ at the age of twenty-eight.
2. Catherine decided to go to Avignon to persuade the pope to return to Rome, a cause started by Saint Bridget of Sweden in 1367. (Note: From 1309-1377—throughout the leadership of seven popes—the papacy was in Avignon, France, rather than Rome. This period of sixty-eight years is known as the Avignon Captivity or the Babylonian Captivity—as it was for the same length of time as the exile of the Jewish people in Babylon from 605 BC to 537 BC.)

Chapter 8—In Which Catherine Persuades the Holy Father to Return the Papacy to Rome

1. Catherine felt that Rome was where the pope belonged, as for hundreds of years it was the city of the papacy. Since 1375, the Republic of Florence was at war with Pope Gregory XI. Catherine was hopeful that the pope's return to Rome would help bring peace and save lives.
2. In her attempt to get the pope to return to Rome, Catherine prayed and made sacrifices. She wrote long letters to the pope.
3. Catherine's humility when she spoke to the pope, her statement that it was not she but God who urged him to return, and his confirmation of her stigmata all helped convince Gregory XI that that he should return to Rome.

Chapter 9—In Which Catherine's Suffering Ends

1. Jesus promised Catherine that no one in her house would go to hell and that her mother would not be taken from this world against her own will (unprepared).
2. Due to Catherine's urging, Pope Gregory XI returned to Rome, only to die two years later. After his death, two elections were held to replace him, and two popes claimed to be the true pope—a Frenchman and an Italian. Many people felt that if Catherine had not urged Pope Gregory

to return to Rome, the double election never would have taken place. Catherine assumed the responsibility for this decision and viewed herself as a failure because of it. (This event in our Church's history is known as the Great Schism and lasted until 1414.)

3. Catherine had always done the most important thing—she had always loved God and carried out His Holy Will.

Answer Key to Book Summary Test

1. Miracles attributed to Catherine in her lifetime include the following: at least three visions of our Lord and the saints, her hearing the voice of our Lord, the elevation of Catherine above the ground in the cave, the rapid transportation of Catherine home after her day of being a hermit, the appearance of the dove above her head while she was at prayer, the teaching of reading and writing to Catherine by our Lord, the vision in which our Lord gave a wedding ring to her, the appearance of our Lord to Catherine in her room to speak to her about her mission, her cure of leprosy, the demonstration to her of the beauty of a soul in the state of sanctifying grace, the appearance of the stigmata on Catherine, her ability to live without drink or food other than Holy Communion, her ability to persuade Pope Gregory XI to return the papacy to Rome, the return of Lapa from the dead due to Catherine's intercession, and the prophecy of Catherine of the time of her own death.

2. Catherine belonged to the order of the Dominicans as a tertiary or lay Dominican.

3. The daily life of Catherine in her late teens and twenties consisted of much prayer and seclusion with many corporal works of mercy within her home and throughout the community. She spent three years (from the ages of sixteen to nineteen) within the confines of her bedroom at home praying and offering sacrifices for sinners, only coming out to attend Mass and receive the other sacraments. From the age of nineteen to her death at the age of thirty-three, she performed works of mercy—spiritual and corporal—caring for the sick, visiting those in prison, bringing food to the hungry, and causing many

to return to the Faith through the Sacrament of Penance or Reconciliation.

4. When she traveled to France, St. Catherine of Siena finished the work started by Saint Bridget and many others by persuading Pope Gregory XI to return to Rome—thus ending the sixty-eight-year pontifical reign in Avignon, France.

5. Answers will vary.

R ead

A loud

C urriculum

E nrichment

For

H istory Enhancement

E xamples of Saintly Lives

A lternative Book Reports

V ocabulary

E xpository Writing

N ourishment in the Catholic Faith

Other RACE for Heaven Products

RACE for Heaven study guides use Mary Fabyan Windeatt's saint biographies to teach the Catholic faith to all members of your family. Written with your family's various learning levels in mind, these flexible study guides succeed as stand-alone unit studies or supplements to your regular curriculum. Thirty to sixty minutes per day will allow your family to experience:

- ☑ The spirituality and holy habits of the saints
- ☑ Lively family discussions on important faith topics
- ☑ Increased critical thinking and reading comprehension skills
- ☑ Quality read-aloud time with Catholic "living books"
- ☑ Enhanced knowledge of Catholic doctrine and the Bible
- ☑ History and geography incorporated into saintly literature
- ☑ Writing projects based on secular and Catholic historical events and characters respond request

Purchase these guides individually or in the following grade-level packages (Grades are determined solely on the length of each book in the series.):

Grades 3-4: *St. Thomas Aquinas, The Story of the "Dumb Ox"*; *St. Catherine of Siena, The Girl Who Saw Saints in the Sky*; *Patron Saint of First Communicants, The Story of Blessed Imelda Lambertini;* and *The Miraculous Medal, The Story of Our Lady's Appearances to St. Catherine Labouré*

Grade 5: *St. Rose, First Canonized Saint of the Americas; St. Martin de Porres, The Story of the Little Doctor of Lima, Peru; King David and His Songs, A Story of the Psalms;* and *Blessed Marie of New France, The Story of the First Missionary Sisters in Canada*

Grade 6: *St. Dominic, Preacher of the Rosary and Founder of the Dominicans; St. Benedict, The Story of the Father of the Western Monks; The Children of Fatima and Our Lady's Message to the World;* and *St. John Masias, Marvelous Dominican Gatekeeper of Lima, Peru*

Grade 7: *The Little Flower, The Story of St. Therese of the Child Jesus; St. Hyacinth, The Story of the Apostle of the North; Curé of Ars, The Story of St. John Vianney, Patron Saint of Parish Priests;* and *St. Louis de Montfort, The Story of Our Lady's Slave*

Grade 8: *Pauline Jaricot, Foundress of the Living Rosary and the Society for the Propagation of Faith; St. Francis Solano, Wonder-Worker of the New World and Apostle of Argentina & Peru; St. Paul the Apostle, The Story of the Apostle to the Gentiles;* and *St. Margaret Mary, Apostle of the Sacred Heart*

The Windeatt Dictionary: Pre-Vatican II Terms and Catholic Words from Mary Fabyan Windeatt's Saint Biographies explains over 450 Catholic terms and expressions used in this popular saint biography series. Indispensable in expanding knowledge and practice of the Catholic faith, this book provides a ready access for the Catholic vocabulary words used in the RACE for Heaven Windeatt study guides. This dictionary also includes a Catholic book report resource that contains suggestions for forty-five Catholic book reports: fourteen writing projects, ten book report activities, and twenty-one topics for saint biographies.

Graced Encounters with Mary Fabyan Windeatt's Saints: 344 Ways to Imitate the Holy Habits of the Saints is a compilation of the "Growing in Holiness" sections of RACE for Heaven's Catholic study guides for the Windeatt saint biography series and presents 344 examples of saintly behavior, one for nearly every chapter in each of these twenty biographies. Enhance your encounter with the saints by practicing the models of devotion, service, penance, prayer, and virtue offered in this guide.

Communion with the Saints: A Family Preparation Program for First Communion and Beyond in the Spirit of St. Therese imitates St. Therese of the Child Jesus and her family who studied and prayed for sixty-nine days in anticipation of Therese's First Holy Communion. Modeling this preparation, the *Communion with the Saints* program will help any family find renewed fervor in the reception of the Eucharist. This resource includes a chapter-by-chapter study of the following four books:

- *The Little Flower, The Story of Saint Therese of the Child Jesus*—to provide the foundation of God's love for us and to encourage a desire for holiness
- *The Children of Fatima and Our Lady's Message to the World*—to show the sinfulness of our world and the need to avoid sin
- *The Patron Saint of First Communicants, The Story of Blessed Imelda Lambertini*—to inspire devotion to the Sacrament of Holy Communion
- *The King of the Golden City* by Mother Mary Loyola—to illustrate Jesus' Presence as a source of grace necessary to live a holy life

Each of the sixty-nine days of preparation includes read-aloud selections with enrichment activities, meditational readings, catechism lessons, and plenty of practical application to promote a growth in holiness and sanctity. Weekend suggestions include a list of over thirty-five family projects. The use of *My First Communion Journal* is encouraged with this program.

My First Communion Journal in Imitation of Saint Therese of the Child Jesus provides a lasting keepsake of a child's First Holy Communion. Saint Therese of the Child Jesus and her family studied and prayed for sixty-nine days prior to Therese's First Holy Communion. This journal imitates that family model of preparation for the reception of the Most Holy Eucharist. Each daily entry contains a stanza of a poem composed by Saint Therese, a quotation from Saint Faustina Kowalska's diary *(Divine Mercy in My Soul)*, or a Scripture quotation. Two weekly themes—a floral theme in imitation of Saint Therese and a battle theme molded from the teachings of Saint Paul—are offered with accompanying weekly passages from Scripture suitable for memorization. This journal may be completed in conjunction with the *Communion with the Saints* program or used separately.

The King of the Golden City Study Edition is a new edition of a book that was originally published in 1921. This treasure of a book was written in response to a student's appeal for instructions along with "little stories" to help her prepare for Holy Communion. To fulfill this request, Mother Loyola of the Bar Convent in York, England, wrote a simple story that illustrates Jesus' desire to share an intimate relationship with each one of His children. This new edition contains some updated language, but quite deliberately, does not contain any pictures. Readers, as they progress through this story, will form a mental image of their King, one as unique and personal as their own relationship with Him. The study sections assist with the allegory, connect to the Bible as well as to the catechism, and explore the art of prayer in the spirit of the three Carmelite Doctors of the Church. Although written over eighty-five years ago for a young child, this book remains a timeless masterpiece of Catholic literature suitable for all ages.

Reading the Saints: Lists of Catholic Books for Children Plus Book Collecting Tips for the Home and School Library (formerly entitled *Saintly Resources*) is a valuable tool for Catholic home educators, classroom teachers, and collectors of Catholic juvenile books. *Reading the Saints* will help you discover living books from such popular out-of-print Catholic juvenile series as Catholic Treasury, Vision Books, and American Background Books as well as current series books for young Catholics. Use this book to find:

- Over 800 Catholic books listed by author, series, reading level, century, and geographical location
- More than 275 authors of saint biographies, historical fiction, and poetry written for Catholic juvenile readers
- Publishers of Catholic children's books, present and past
- Helpful advice for collecting and caring for used books
- Hundreds of age-appropriate, accessible living books to enrich your study of the Catholic Church's rich heritage of saints and notable Catholic historical figures
- Information on how to build and maintain your own library of Catholic juvenile books
- Inspiring quotations about book collecting, reading, and the love of books

Alternative Book Reports for Catholic Students contains forty-five book report ideas that encourage critical thinking for ages seven to fourteen. These ideas are intended to provoke a reflection on those themes and topics that support and encourage Catholic living as well as some that may conflict with our Faith. Many report topics require an examination of our personal faith life and prompt us to take a lesson from the book to strengthen our own faith in God. Activities vary from written exercises to creative art projects and include twenty-one topics specifically designed for saint biographies. Other activities can be used within a group or family.

The Outlaws of Ravenhurst Study Edition contains a classic story of the persecution of Scottish Catholics that was first written in 1923 and was revised and reprinted in 1950. This 2009 edition of Sr. Mary Imelda Wallace's *Outlaws of Ravenhurst* contains the revised story of 1950 plus chapter-by-chapter aids to assist readers in assimilating the book's strong Catholic elements into their own lives. The study section focuses on critical thinking, integration of Biblical teachings, and the study of the virtuous life to which Christ calls us as mature Catholics. With its emphasis on virtues (theological and moral plus the gifts and fruits of the Holy Spirit), the spiritual and corporal works of mercy, and the Beatitudes, *Outlaws of Ravenhurst Study Edition* is a fun and effective catechetical tool for Catholics preparing for the Sacrament of Confirmation.

To Order: Email race4hvn@hughes.net or order at RaceforHeaven.com. MasterCard, VISA, Discover, American Express, Paypal, checks, and money orders accepted.

CPSIA information can be obtained at www.ICGtesting.com
Printed in the USA
LVOW05s0720300314

379383LV00003B/357/P

9 781934 185117